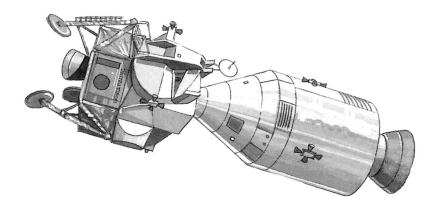

Author:

Ian Graham was born in Belfast in 1953. He studied applied physics at City University, London, where he later earned a postgraduate degree in journalism, specializing in science and technology. He has written more than one hundred children's nonfiction books and numerous magazine articles.

Artist:

David Antram was born in Brighton, England, in 1958. He studied at Eastbourne College of Art and then worked in advertising for fifteen years before becoming a full-time artist. He has illustrated many children's nonfiction books.

Series Creator:

David Salariya was born in Dundee, Scotland. He has illustrated a wide range of books and has created and designed many new series for publishers both in the U.K. and overseas. In 1989, he established The Salariya Book Company. He lives in Brighton with his wife, illustrator Shirley Willis, and their son Jonathan.

Editor:

Karen Barker Smith

Created, designed, and produced by
The Salariya Book Company Ltd
Book House, 25 Marlborough Place
Brighton BN1 1UB

Please visit The Salariya Book Company at:
www.salariya.com

ISBN 0-531-12311-1 (Lib. Bdg.)
ISBN 0-531-16650-3 (Pbk.)

Published in the United States by Franklin Watts
A Division of Scholastic Inc.
90 Sherman Turnpike, Danbury, CT 06816

A CIP catalog record for this title is available from the Library of Congress.

Printed and bound in China.

Printed on paper from sustainable forests.

You Wouldn't Want to Be on Apollo 13!

I'm sure 13 is an unlucky number!

A Mission You'd Rather Not Go On

Written by
Ian Graham

Illustrated by
David Antram

Created and designed by
David Salariya

W
FRANKLIN WATTS
A Division of Scholastic Inc.
NEW YORK • TORONTO • LONDON • AUCKLAND • SYDNEY
MEXICO CITY • NEW DELHI • HONG KONG
DANBURY, CONNECTICUT

Contents

Introduction   5

Practice Makes Perfect   6

The Apollo Spacecraft   8

Launch Day   10

Liftoff!   12

Goodbye Earth   14

Living in a Tin Can   16

Houston, We've Had a Problem   18

Failure Is Not an Option   20

Cold, Wet, and Stuffy   22

Lost Mission   24

Going Home   26

Down to Earth   28

Glossary   30

Index   32

Introduction

It is April 1970. You are an astronaut that is about to climb into a spacecraft and fly to the Moon. You have been training for years for the chance to take part in this mission. You watched two members of the *Apollo 11* crew, Neil Armstrong and Buzz Aldrin, become the first people to walk on another world. They landed on the Moon on July 20, 1969. Charles Conrad and Alan Bean of the *Apollo 12* mission also landed on the Moon in November of that year. The whole world watched them explore the Moon on television.

Now it is your turn. You are a member of the three-man crew of *Apollo 13*. Some people think that 13 is an unlucky number — you don't know it yet, but *Apollo 13* will be an incredibly unlucky mission. On your way to the Moon, your spacecraft will suffer the most serious accident to happen during a moon landing mission. It is so serious that no one knows if you will be able to get back to Earth. Your fate depends on hundreds of engineers on Earth working out a way to get you home safely. You wouldn't want to be on *Apollo 13*!

Practice Makes Perfect

The whole crew practices everything that you will have to do during the mission. You do it over and over again until you could do it in your sleep. You train in simulators that look exactly like the real spacecraft. The mission controllers keep you on your toes by surprising you with all sorts of emergencies to see how well you deal with them. If you are going to make a mistake, it is better to do it in the simulator than on the way to the Moon. By the time launch day comes you have to know the spacecraft inside out, be able to fly it perfectly, and know what to do in any situation.

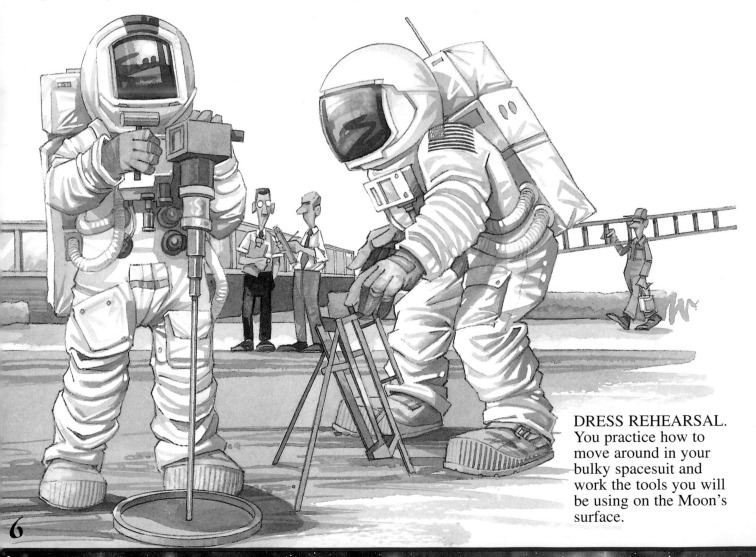

DRESS REHEARSAL. You practice how to move around in your bulky spacesuit and work the tools you will be using on the Moon's surface.

Handy Hint

Remember to lock your spacesuit helmet firmly in place before you are lowered into the water tank for a training session!

FLYING SPIDER. You practice flying a spider-like jet-craft designed to fly exactly like the Apollo Lunar Module.

WEIGHTLESSNESS is simulated in a training airplane (left). So many people get airsick in this plane that it is nicknamed the "Vomit Comet!"

ON THE MOON, you will weigh one sixth as much as you weigh on Earth because the Moon has less gravity. You are hung sideways so that you can see what it is like to weigh so little (right).

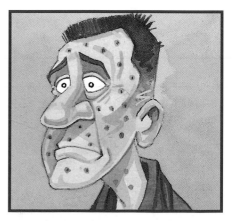

UNDERWATER. You practice making spacewalks in a huge water tank (left). The uplift you get from the water provides the closest thing to weightlessness on Earth.

BUG ALERT! Someone the crew works with catches German measles. To avoid becoming ill in space, one crew member with no immunity to the disease is replaced two days before launch.

The Apollo Spacecraft

The week before launch you visit the giant Vehicle Assembly Building at Cape Canaveral, Florida, to watch the Apollo spacecraft being hoisted on top of its rocket. The spacecraft is made of three parts, or modules: the Command Module, the Service Module, and the Lunar Module. Every Apollo crew gives its Command and Lunar Modules names. For *Apollo 13*, the Command Module is called *Odyssey* and the Lunar Module is called *Aquarius*.

Saturn V is the biggest rocket ever to launch people into space. It is actually three rockets, called stages, stacked on top of each other. As each stage uses up its fuel, it falls off and the next stage takes over.

Saturn V rocket

Launch escape system

Boost protective cover

364 feet (111 m)

GIANT LAUNCHER. The huge Saturn V rocket stands 364 feet (111 m) from the base of its first-stage engines to the tip of the Apollo spacecraft at the top. It will be launched 13 times and is successful every time.

USA

USA

UNITED STATES

I'm glad it won't be me sitting at the top of this thing!

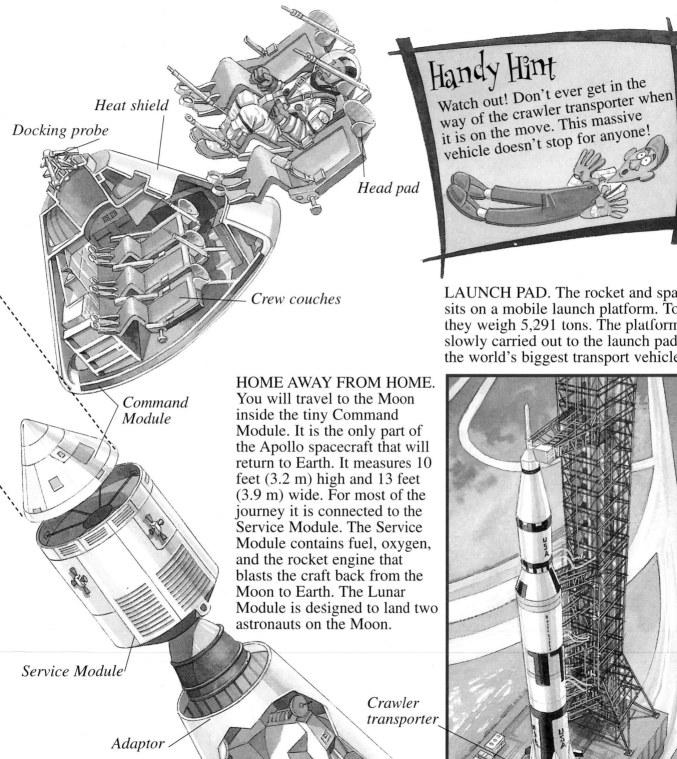

Heat shield

Docking probe

Head pad

Crew couches

Command
Module

Service Module

Adaptor

Lunar Module

Handy Hint

Watch out! Don't ever get in the way of the crawler transporter when it is on the move. This massive vehicle doesn't stop for anyone!

LAUNCH PAD. The rocket and spacecraft sits on a mobile launch platform. Together they weigh 5,291 tons. The platform is slowly carried out to the launch pad by the world's biggest transport vehicle.

HOME AWAY FROM HOME. You will travel to the Moon inside the tiny Command Module. It is the only part of the Apollo spacecraft that will return to Earth. It measures 10 feet (3.2 m) high and 13 feet (3.9 m) wide. For most of the journey it is connected to the Service Module. The Service Module contains fuel, oxygen, and the rocket engine that blasts the craft back from the Moon to Earth. The Lunar Module is designed to land two astronauts on the Moon.

Crawler transporter

9

Launch Day
Countdown to Takeoff

WAKE UP! You are called exactly four hours and 17 minutes before launch.

SAY AH. The flight doctor gives you a final once-over four hours and two minutes before launch to make sure you are in top condition.

Launch day has arrived. It is April 11, 1970. Your 248,548-mile (400,000-km) journey to the Moon begins a few hours from now with a trip into orbit around the Earth. While you and the rest of the crew go through your preparations for takeoff, a team of engineers get the spacecraft and its mighty rocket ready for you. You can't waste any time. Everything, from filling the rocket's fuel tanks to having your breakfast, has its own time slot in the carefully planned countdown. It's too late to change your mind now!

BREAKFAST. Exactly three hours and 32 minutes before launch you have breakfast — steak, eggs, orange juice, coffee, and toast — and then put on your spacesuit.

SNOOPY CAP. This soft cap (4) contains earpieces and a microphone for radio communications. A clear "fishbowl" helmet (5) locks onto the top of the suit and gloves lock onto metal rings at the ends of the sleeves (6).

SUITING UP. The various parts of the spacesuit are put on in order. Electrodes (1) are glued to your chest to monitor your heartbeat. Underwear — a pair of "long johns" (2) — is the first layer next to your skin. Next, you pull on the spacesuit legs, push your head through the neck ring, and pull on the body and arms (3).

Helmet

Mission badge

Watch

Boots

I'm suited up and ready to go!

Handy Hint

If you need to scratch your nose or sneeze, do it BEFORE your helmet is fitted! You can't take your helmet off again until you are in orbit.

ALL ABOARD. Three hours and seven minutes before launch you board the crew transfer van. You arrive at launch pad 39A, 12 minutes later.

GOING UP. You take an elevator to the top of the launch tower and walk across the access arm into the white room next to the Command Module. The white room team is waiting for you.

TAKE A SEAT. You board the spacecraft 2 hours and 40 minutes before launch. Take care not to snag your spacesuit as you slide through the hatch. Each one costs $1.5 million!

11

Liftoff!

When the countdown reaches zero, you start a 12-minute rollercoaster ride through Earth's atmosphere. As the rocket leaves the launchpad, the time on the clock at Mission Control in Houston, Texas, is 13:13, which is military time for 1:13 PM. Pictures of the soaring rocket and its flight path appear on a big display screen at Mission Control.

T (TAKEOFF) –3 MINUTES, 7 SECONDS. The Saturn V rocket is given the firing command that starts its automatic launch sequence. Computers start its fuel pumps.

T –8.9 SECONDS. The first-stage engines fire. The rocket is held down on the launch-pad until all five engines are running.

ZERO. *Apollo 13* and the 3,300-ton Saturn V launch-rocket gently lift off the launchpad.

RROOARR

Apollo 13's bad luck first strikes when one of the rocket engines shuts down two minutes early. For a few moments you don't know if Apollo 13 will make it into space. The remaining engines fire longer to make up for the problem. Engineers at Mission Control check to see if there is enough fuel left to send the spacecraft to the Moon.

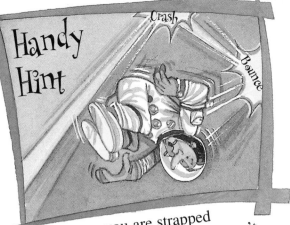

Handy Hint

Crash

Bounce

Make sure you are strapped tightly into your seat. If you aren't, you will bounce around the Command Module like a cork in a bottle when the rocket blasts off!

T +3 MINUTES, 20 SECONDS. The launch escape tower's rockets fire, carrying the tower and boost protective cover away from the top of the spacecraft.

T +2 MINUTES, 44 SECONDS. The empty first stage falls off and 2 seconds later the second-stage engines fire.

T +12 MINUTES, 39 SECONDS. The spacecraft is safely in orbit around Earth. Time to check that everything is working properly.

T +9 MINUTES, 53 SECONDS. The empty second stage falls off. The third-stage engines fire three seconds later.

13

Goodbye Earth

The spacecraft checks out fine so you get the go-ahead to fire the third-stage engine and head for the Moon. The engine boosts your speed from 17,398 miles per hour (28,000 kph) to the 24,854 mph (40,000 kph) needed to break away from Earth's gravity. Once you are safely on your way to the Moon, there is a very important job to do. The Lunar Module is packed inside the top of the rocket, underneath the Command and Service Modules (CSM). The CSM has to be separated from the rocket and turned around so that it can pull the Lunar Module out. This delicate maneuver requires pinpoint flying. Nothing less will do.

STEADY AS YOU GO. Thrusters nudge the spacecraft slowly forward and away from the end of Saturn V's third stage (above).

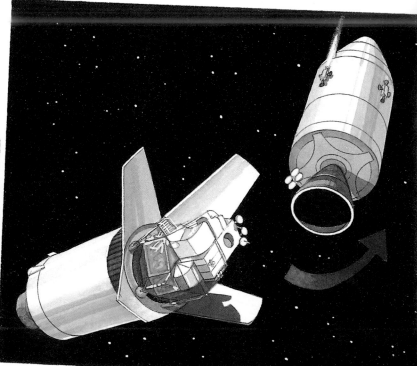

TURNAROUND. The thrusters are fired again to turn the spacecraft around. The end of the rocket opens up like a giant flower, revealing the Lunar Module (above).

STEERING. You steer the spacecraft by using hand controllers to fire rocket thrusters on the Service Module.

Piece of cake!

Handy Hint

If you suffer from space sickness, grab a bag fast. Remember, during weightlessness EVERYTHING floats around the spacecraft — yuck!

Docking probe

DOCKING. The CSM eases forward and docks with the Lunar Module (above). A probe on top of the CSM fits into a hole on top of the Lunar Module, and the two crafts lock together.

EASY DOES IT. The CSM slowly backs up and pulls the Lunar Module out of the end of the rocket (above). It all goes perfectly. You are on your way.

15

Living in a Tin Can

Being an Apollo astronaut sometimes feels like living inside a tiny tin can. You have to get along with two other people in a small space for more than a week. You also have to get used to noise all the time. The spacecraft is never completely silent. There is the hum of air pumps, voices on the radio, and the sounds of other crew members moving about. The temperature is kept at a steady 71.6 °F (22°C) so once you're in orbit you can take off the bulky spacesuit you wore for the launch and put on a more comfortable flight suit. In orbit you experience weightlessness and can float around inside the spacecraft.

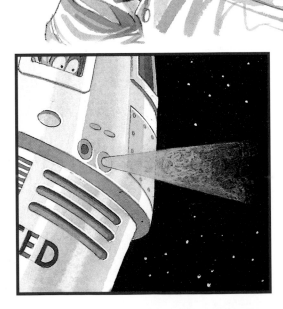

SPACE FOOD. You wish you could eat "normal" food. Most space food is dried to save weight in the spacecraft (left). You add water to make it edible.

USING THE TOILET. Three astronauts produce a lot of urine during a mission. To save weight it is dumped overboard (right).

There is no "up" or "down" in space. You can work just as easily standing on your head as with your feet on the floor.

Be careful where you're floating!

THE BARBECUE ROLL. The spacecraft spins constantly, very slowly, so that it is heated evenly by the Sun (left).

TV STAR. You present television reports, or telecasts, from the spacecraft to show viewers how the flight is going (right).

17

Houston, We've Had a Problem

n April 13th, *Apollo 13* is 204,431 miles (329,000 km) away from Earth. Each day the moon looks bigger through the Command Module windows. Mission Control asks you to turn on fans inside the Service Module's oxygen tanks. As soon as the switch is hit, you hear a loud bang. You watch your instruments in horror. The spacecraft seems to be losing oxygen and electrical power. You struggle to understand what has happened. Mission controllers on Earth can't believe what they see on their computer screens.

Disaster Strikes

1. THE JOLT. You hear a bang and the spacecraft shakes violently. You think it might have been hit by a piece of space rock.

What was that?!

2. ALARMS go off in the spacecraft and at Mission Control. You watch your instruments in disbelief.

3. WHAT'S HAPPENING? Mission controllers think their computers have gone crazy. Their screens don't seem to make sense.

4. GAS ESCAPE. You look through a window and see something spraying out into space. It must be oxygen!

5. LOSING POWER. Your instruments show that the Command Module's fuel cells are losing power fast.

6. MOVE OUT! You quickly power down the Command Module and move into the Lunar Module so that you can use its air and electricity.

BANG!!

WHAT HAPPENED? Later, it is discovered that an electrical fault blew up an oxygen tank and damaged equipment in the Service Module.

19

Failure Is Not an Option

At Mission Control, the flight director tells everyone to find a way to get the crew home. He shouts, "Failure is not an option!" Ground controllers and engineers immediately start discussing what to do. Some of them want to turn the spacecraft around and bring it straight back to Earth. Others want to let the spacecraft keep going and use the Moon's gravity to swing it around and back to Earth. This option would take longer. The long way would be less risky but no one knows if the spacecraft's oxygen and electricity will last long enough. You keep calling Mission Control but they are still making a decision.

Option One

The spacecraft does a U-turn and comes straight home. It gets you home fast, but you would have to fire the Service Module engine. It might be damaged, it might not work, and it might explode.

Watch your instruments like a hawk. They tell you exactly what is happening in the rest of the spacecraft, especially all the parts that you can't see.

Those are our options, gentlemen. Let's get those astronauts home safely.

Option Two

Mission controllers decide it is safer to go to the Moon and swing behind it. You can use the Lunar Module engine to stay on course, but it wasn't designed for this. Will this plan work?

Cold, Wet, and Stuffy

Keeping warm is not as important as getting home alive, so the spacecraft heaters are switched off to save electricity. The temperature falls to just above freezing. Moisture from your breath condenses on the cold instrument panels, walls, and windows. The whole spacecraft is wet. It is also dark because most of the lights are switched off. It gets very stuffy — the Lunar Module was designed for two astronauts, not three, so it can't purify the air fast enough. The carbon dioxide in the air rises to a dangerous level. If it continues to rise you will lose consciousness! You have to do something about it.

A Bit of Do-it-Yourself

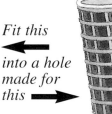

Fit this ← *into a hole made for this* →

THE COMMAND MODULE has air purifier canisters that could freshen the air, but they are square. The fittings in the Lunar Module are round. You make them fit by using pieces of hose, sticky tape, plastic bags, and rubber bands. It works! The amount of carbon dioxide in the air starts falling.

A Wee Problem

The crippled spacecraft is so hard to control that you have to stop dumping urine overboard. When it sprays out into space it pushes the spacecraft off course. You have to save it all in plastic bags and store them inside the spacecraft!

shiver

Lost Mission

If everything had gone as planned, *Apollo 13* would have landed on part of the Moon called Fra Mauro. *Apollo 11* landed in the Sea of Tranquillity and *Apollo 12* landed in the Ocean of Storms. The ground in these two locations was flat because lava had flowed over the areas. Scientists wanted samples of older rocks from the hills and mountains that hadn't been covered by lava, but these places are more dangerous to land on. The earlier missions proved that astronauts could fly the Lunar Module manually and choose a safe landing spot. It was decided that *Aquarius* from *Apollo 13* would land in the Fra Mauro hills.

If Nothing Had Gone Wrong...

SPACESUIT. The spacesuit you would have worn on the Moon (right) has extra-tough gloves, boots, and a visor over the helmet to keep your head cool. You would also have worn a backpack with oxygen and a radio.

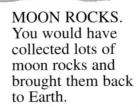

MOON ROCKS. You would have collected lots of moon rocks and brought them back to Earth.

HEAT FLOW. You would have drilled holes in the Moon's surface to test how heat flows through it.

Handy Hint

Be careful not to fall over on your back or you could be stranded there. You would not be able to get up because of the Moon's low gravity.

What a fantastic view!

SOLAR WIND. You would have collected samples of the solar wind – particles that stream out of the Sun and hit the Moon.

PHOTOGRAPHY. You would have taken thousands of close-up photographs of dust, rocks, and craters on the Moon's surface.

MOONQUAKES. You were planning to put instruments on the Moon's surface to detect the vibrations of moonquakes.

LONE ORBITER. While two astronauts explored the surface, the third would orbit the Moon alone in the Command Module.

Going Home

Lunar Module

Command and Service Module (CSM)

You receive new instructions from Mission Control. You are to fire the Lunar Module's descent stage engine to change course. If it works it will send you around the Moon and back to Earth. Although, this engine was not designed to be used like this. It is the engine that would have slowed the Lunar Module down as it approached the Moon's surface. The engine has to be fired before you reach the Moon and again just after you reappear from behind it. While you are behind the Moon you are out of contact with Mission Control. If something goes wrong no one can help you.

NERVOUS WAIT. As the spacecraft disappears behind the Moon, everyone in Mission Control can only wait and hope that the burn (the firing of the engine) has gone well.

WHAT A VIEW! You gaze out of the Lunar Module's windows at the Moon as you fly over your landing site at Fra Mauro. Earth slips out of sight as you fly behind the Moon.

Handy Hint

Remember to close the Command Module hatch before you undock the Lunar Module and cast it adrift. Otherwise you will be sucked out into space!

That would've been a great place to visit.

BURN 1. The Lunar Module engine fires perfectly for 35 seconds, speeding you on your way behind the Moon.

FIRST SIGHT. When the Service Module is finally cast adrift, you gasp as you catch your first sight of the damage (left). The explosion has blown out one side of the module.

BURN 2. You fire the Lunar Module engine again for four minutes to speed up your return flight to Earth (above).

GOODBYE LUNAR MODULE. You power up the damp, cold, and dark Command Module and prepare for your return to Earth. You cast the Lunar Module adrift (right) and say goodbye to the craft that acted as your lifeboat.

27

Down to Earth

You are nearly home but you still face the most dangerous part of the mission – re-entering the Earth's atmosphere. It is very important to keep the spacecraft on course so that it hits the atmosphere at the right angle. If it comes in at the wrong angle it will either burn up or bounce off.

The heat shield glows red hot. It is all that stands between you and the extreme heat outside. No one knows if it was damaged by the explosion. The air around the spacecraft gets so hot that radio waves can't get through. You can't talk to Mission Control and they can't hear you. They do not know if you are alive or dead.

TOO SHALLOW. A spacecraft hitting Earth's atmosphere at too shallow an angle would bounce off it like a stone skipping across water.

TOO STEEP. If the Command Module dives into the atmosphere at too steep of an angle, it will get too hot and burn up.

CHUTES OPEN. The Command Module falls through the clouds and floats down under three huge parachutes.

Handy Hint

When you step out onto the deck of the recovery ship don't get too close to anyone — remember, you haven't had a bath for a whole week!

WELCOME HOME. You step out of the helicopter onto the deck of the recovery ship and wave to the crew and cameras.

"13 CALLING." Cheering breaks out at Mission Control as the radio crackles and you report in (above).

SPLASHDOWN. The module hits the ocean with a splash (below left). You are safely back on Earth.

DIVERS KNOCK on the spacecraft hatch (below) and help you out to a waiting helicopter.

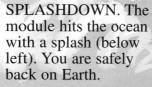

29

Glossary

Boost protective cover The cover that protected the Apollo Command Module during launch.

Burn A short firing of a rocket engine to change a spacecraft's course.

Canisters A container, usually made of metal.

Cape Canaveral A place in Florida, where the John F. Kennedy Space Center is located. Many space flights are launched from there.

Carbon dioxide A gas that is breathed out by people.

Command Module The cone-shaped part of an Apollo spacecraft where the crew lived.

Crawler transporter A giant vehicle that moves rockets from their assembly building to the launchpad.

CSM The Command and Service Module, a spacecraft made from the Command Module and Service Module linked together.

Fuel cell A device that uses oxygen and hydrogen gases to make electricity and water.

Gravity The force that pulls everything toward a large object such as a planet or moon.

Hatch A doorway in a spacecraft.

Heat shield The part of a spacecraft that protects the rest of the craft from the heat of re-entry.

Launch escape tower A rocket designed to fly the Command Module away to safety in an emergency during launch.

Lava Molten rock that flows out onto the surface of a planet or moon.

Lunar Module The part of an Apollo spacecraft designed to land on the Moon.

Manually Done by hand instead of being done automatically by machines.

Mission Control The building where space flights are monitored and managed.

Orbit To travel in a circle around a planet or moon.

Oxygen A gas humans breathe.

Particle An extremely small piece or speck of something.

Recovery ship A ship sent to where a spacecraft is expected to land to pick up the crew.

Re-entry Coming back into the Earth's atmosphere from space.

Service Module The part of the Apollo spacecraft that supplied the Command Module with oxygen, water, electricity, and rocket power.

Simulator A machine made to look like a vehicle, such as a spacecraft, used to train pilots.

Stage Part of a larger rocket with its own engine or engines, that falls off when its fuel is used up.

Thruster A small rocket engine used to adjust the position of a spacecraft while in space.

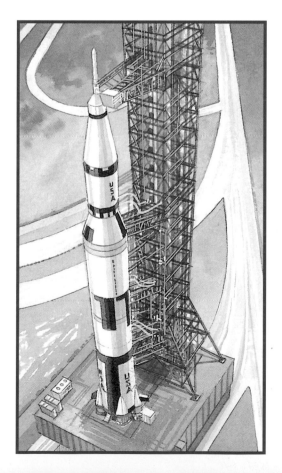

Index

A
access arm 11
air purifiers 22
Aldrin, Buzz 5
Aquarius 8, 24
Armstrong, Neil 5
astronaut 5, 8, 9, 16, 22, 25
atmosphere 10, 28, 31
automatic launch sequence 12

B
barbecue roll 17
Bean, Alan 5
boost protective cover 13, 30

C
Cape Canaveral 8, 30
carbon dioxide 22, 30
Command Module (CM) 8, 9, 11, 13, 14, 18, 19, 25-28, 30
Conrad, Charles 5
crawler transporter 9, 30
CSM (Command and Service Module) 14, 15, 30

F
flight director 20
flight suit 16
food 10, 16
Fra Mauro 24, 26
fuel 8-10, 13
fuel cells 19, 30

G
gravity 14, 20, 30

H
hand controllers 15
heat shield 9, 28, 30
helmet 7, 10, 11

I
illness 7

L
launch 10, 11, 16
launch escape tower 13, 31
launchpad 9, 11, 12
lava 24, 31
Lunar Module 7-9, 14, 15, 19, 21, 22, 24, 26, 27, 31

M
Mission Control 12, 13, 18, 20, 21, 26, 29, 31
mobile launch platform 9
moon 5-7, 9, 10, 13, 14, 18, 20, 21, 24-27
moonquakes 25
moon rocks 24

O
Odyssey 8
orbit 10, 11, 13, 16, 25, 31
oxygen 9, 18-20, 31

P
parachutes 29

R
recovery ship 29, 31
re-entry 28, 31
rocket 8-9, 10, 12-13, 14
rocket stage 8, 12, 13, 26

S
Saturn V 8, 12, 14
Service Module (SM) 8, 9, 14, 15, 18-20, 27, 31
simulator 6, 31
solar wind 25
space sickness 15
spacesuit 6, 7, 10, 11, 16, 24
splashdown 29
stage 8, 12, 13, 31

T
takeoff 10, 12
telecasts 17
temperature 16, 22
thrusters 14, 31
toilet 16
training 6-7

V
Vehicle Assembly Building 8
"Vomit Comet" 7

W
weightlessness 7, 16